Concept Cars

BY DENNY VON FINN

BELLWETHER MEDIA • MINNEAPOLIS, MN

TORQUE™

Are you ready to take it to the extreme?

Torque books thrust you into the action-packed world of sports, vehicles, and adventure. These books may include dirt, smoke, fire, and dangerous stunts.

WARNING: READ AT YOUR OWN RISK.

This edition first published in 2010 by Bellwether Media, Inc.

No part of this publication may be reproduced in whole or in part without written permission of the publisher. For information regarding permission, write to Bellwether Media, Inc., Attention: Permissions Department, Post Office Box 19349, Minneapolis, MN 55419.

Library of Congress Cataloging-in-Publication Data
Von Finn, Denny.
  Concept cars / by Denny Von Finn.
      p. cm. — (Torque. Cool rides)
  Includes bibliographical references and index.
  Summary: "Amazing photography accompanies engaging information about concept cars. The combination of high-interest subject matter and light text is intended for students in grades 3 through 7"—Provided by publisher.
  ISBN 978-1-60014-276-5 (hardcover : alk. paper)
  1. Experimental automobiles—Juvenile literature. 2. Experimental automobiles—Pictorial works—Juvenile literature. I. Title.
  TL147.V66 2010
  629.2'3—dc22
                              2009008481

Printed in the United States of America.

Contents

What Is a Concept Car?

A concept car looks different from a normal car. It has extreme designs and cutting-edge technologies. It is a **prototype** built to show new ideas. In fact, concept means "idea."

Each year automakers introduce new concept cars at auto shows. Concept cars give **consumers** their first look at an automaker's new ideas. Automakers watch how people react to concept cars. They use the features that consumers like best in **production vehicles**. Sometimes a concept car becomes the basis for a production vehicle.

Fast FaCt
The 2007 Honda PUYO concept car featured a glowing body covered in a gel-like material.

ConCept Car History

Early automakers built prototypes to bring in **investors**. In 1896, Henry Ford built a car he called the Quadricycle. Investors formed a company to turn it into a production vehicle.

The first true concept car is credited to a man named Harley Earl. Earl was a **stylist** who worked for General Motors. He oversaw the design of the Buick Y-Job in 1938. Earl's team wanted to know if consumers would like the Y-Job's design.

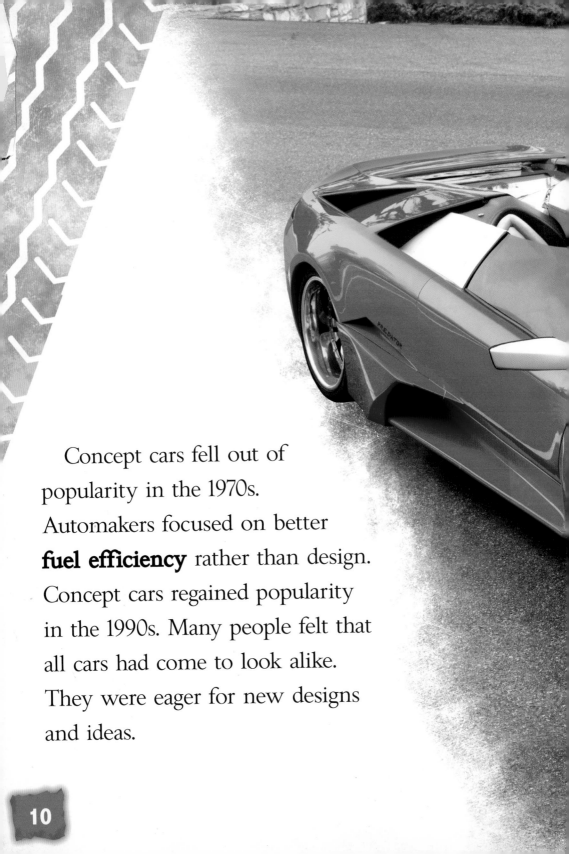

Concept cars fell out of popularity in the 1970s. Automakers focused on better **fuel efficiency** rather than design. Concept cars regained popularity in the 1990s. Many people felt that all cars had come to look alike. They were eager for new designs and ideas.

Fast Fact

The 1958 Ford Nucleon was to be powered by nuclear energy. An operational version was never made.

Designing a Concept Car

It can take months or years to design a concept car. Designers often work in teams. Designers may develop their concepts on paper. They might also mold them from clay. A clay model is called a **mockup**. Most designers also use computers. They use the computer design to build the concept car.

Many concept cars look **futuristic**. This shows people that the car has new features. Cutting-edge materials like **carbon fiber** are often used.

Automakers often use familiar **design cues**.
These are shapes and **lines** the automaker has
used in other cars. These cues make the concept
car look **retro**. They look like new versions of
older cars.

Showing a Concept Car

Concept cars are introduced at auto shows. This is why they are sometimes called show cars. Auto shows are exciting events with flashy displays. Big auto shows are held each year in cities such as Detroit and Los Angeles.

Production vehicles are also introduced at
auto shows. The Chevrolet Volt was shown
in 2008. The Volt is a new **green car** that
is powered by both gasoline and electricity.
The Volt was first introduced as a concept
car in 2007. It can travel 300 miles before
refueling. Its batteries can be recharged by
plugging the car into a normal outlet.

Fast FaCt

Some of the most famous concept cars were introduced at General Motors' Motorama auto show held from 1949 to 1961.

Concept cars are often kept secret until auto shows. This helps create excitement. Automakers always hope for a good reaction when they show the world their new concept cars.

Glossary

carbon fiber—a material made from mixing strong fabric with plastic

consumers—people who buy products, including cars

design cues—familiar elements of a car, such as round taillights or an aggressive grille

fuel efficiency—how much fuel a car uses when driven; a car with poor fuel efficiency uses a lot of fuel.

futuristic—having to do with the future; looking as if from the future.

green car—a car designed to have a small impact on the environment

investors—people who give money to someone with a good idea, expecting to make more money in the future

lines—a word used by designers to help describe a vehicle's shape

mockup—a scale-size model of a concept car, typically made of clay

production vehicles—cars and trucks that automakers manufacture to sell to consumers

prototype—a vehicle built in small numbers to show what a production vehicle might look like

retro—refers to an object that recalls an earlier time period such as the 1950s

stylist—another word for a designer

To Learn More

AT THE LIBRARY

Coughlan, John. *Experimental and Concept Cars.* Minneapolis, Minn.: Capstone, 1994.

Wood, Jonathan. *Concept Cars.* San Diego, Calif.: Thunder Bay Press, 1998.

Zuehlke, Jeffrey. *Concept Cars.* Minneapolis, Minn.: Lerner, 2007.

ON THE WEB

Learning more about concept cars is as easy as 1, 2, 3.

1. Go to www.factsurfer.com.

2. Enter "concept cars" into the search box.

3. Click the "Surf" button and you will see a list of related Web sites.

With factsurfer.com, finding more information is just a click away.

Index

The images in this book are reproduced through the courtesy of: Minik, front cover; Mark Scheuern, pp. 4-5; Paolo Patrizi, p. 7 (top); Ron Kimball / KimballStock, pp. 7 (bottom), 9, 10-11, 14, 15, 18-19, 21; Hulton Archive / Stringer / Getty Images, p. 8; Pgiam, pp. 12-13; Maksim Toome, pp. 16-17; Stan Honda / AFP / Getty Images, pp. 20-21.